Splendid Science

Lynn Huggins-Cooper

In a cave far away, lives a powerful wizard named Whimstaff. He spends his days finding the answers to ancient Science problems and has parchments filled with wonderful words. In this book, Whimstaff shares his knowledge to help you to master the art of Science.

Whimstaff has a goblin assistant named Pointy, who is very clever. Pointy helps Whimstaff perfect his spells and gets annoyed with the laziness of Mugly and Bugly, his fat pet frogs. They spend most of their time eating and sleeping and do as little work as possible.

Pointy also helps Whimstaff look after Miss Snufflebeam, a young dragon who is rather clumsy and often loses Whimstaff's words!

Wizard Whimstaff and his friends are very happy solving Science problems. Join them on a magical quest to win the Trophy of Science Wizardry!

Contents

2	Healthy Habits	18	Gruesome Gases
4	Brilliant Blood	20	Dissolving and Evaporating
6	Dangerous Drugs	22	Spooky States
8	Plant Potions	24	Powerful Planets
10	Seed Sorcery	26	Sensational Sounds
12	Grisly Growing	28	Apprentice Wizard Challenge 2
14	Apprentice Wizard Challenge 1	30	Answers
16	Mucky Micro Organisms	32	Wizard's Trophy of Excellence

Healthy Habits

Welcome, young apprentice! I'm Wizard Whimstaff and I'm here to make you a science wizard! First, I need to teach you about healthy living. To stay healthy, we need to take exercise and eat lots of healthy food like fruit, vegetables, cheese, pasta and rice.

Did you know that the more processed food gets, the less healthy it is? Raw strawberries, for example, are much healthier than strawberry jam. When the fruit is boiled to make jam, it loses vitamins and sugar is added.

Abracadabra!

Task 1 To get you started, look at this banquet menu. Choose the healthiest option for each course, avoiding too much sugary and fatty food!

Starters:
Pastry boats with cheesy sails ☐
Melon with raspberries ☐
Spinach with fried egg centres ☐

Main Course:
Pizza with cheesy chips ☐
Pig pie with creamy buttered potatoes ☐
Pasta with dragon-roasted vegetables ☐
Cheese pasty and chips ☐

Dessert:
Trifle ☐
Banana cream pie ☐
Fruit salad ☐

After Dinner:
Chocolate flake cakes ☐
Chunks of cheese ☐
Grapes and fruit sorbet ☐

Drinks:
Milkshake with ice cream topping ☐
Coffee ☐
Orange juice ☐

Task 2 Look at the foods below. Circle the healthier option.

a cherry pie or cherries?

b lemons or lemon curd?

c cider or apples?

d oranges or orange squash?

e blackberry jam or blackberries?

f potatoes or crisps?

Task 3 Now we need to think about exercise! Tick (✔) the healthier option of each pair. Hey presto!

a ☐ watch TV
  ☐ go jogging

b ☐ walking briskly
  ☐ sitting at a computer

c ☐ sunbathing
  ☐ swimming

d ☐ playing with a games console
  ☐ cycling

Sorcerer's Skill Check

One last task to check your new magical skills. True or false? Write **T** for true and **F** for false.

a Cider is healthier than raw apples.

b Raw food is healthier than processed food.

c Regular exercise is good for you.

d Watching TV is healthier than swimming.

e Regular exercise is bad for you.

Good work brainbox! Time to stick your first silver shield on the trophy at the back of the book.

Brilliant Blood

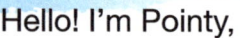

Hello! I'm Pointy, Wizard Whimstaff's helpful assistant. I'm fascinated by the way things work, including me! Did you know that you get out of breath when you exercise, because your muscles are using up lots of oxygen? That makes you breathe faster and your lungs take in more oxygen for your body to use.

And did you know that the oxygen dissolves in your blood, to be taken to all parts of your body? Blood carries goodness from your food and helps get rid of waste too. Your body is amazing!

Task 1 Answer the questions, filling the gaps with the words from the box below. It's easy when you know how!

> blood   oxygen   lungs   dissolves   muscles   breathe

a Blood carries ⟨_____⟩ to all parts of your body.

b Our ⟨_____⟩ use up oxygen as we exercise. That makes us puff!

c ⟨_____⟩ carries oxygen, goodness from food and waste around our bodies.

d Oxygen ⟨_____⟩ in blood.

e We ⟨_____⟩ faster when we take exercise, because our bodies need more oxygen.

f We take in oxygen through our ⟨_____⟩ when we breathe.

Task 2 Super! Look at the pairs of pictures below. Circle the one showing the harder exercise that would make you puff the most.

a

Miss Snufflebeam playing Nintendo™

Pointy cycling

b

Pointy running

Whimstaff watching TV

c

Mugly and Bugly dozing

Miss Snufflebeam playing football with Pointy

Dangerous Drugs

Oh dear! My name's Miss Snufflebeam and I get very confused when I'm explaining things! I've been reading some leaflets I got from school about drugs and medicine, tobacco and alcohol. It's very difficult to understand, but Pointy has explained it all to me!

Medicines can make us better when we are sick, if they are given to us by adults who know what they are doing! Pointy said that a drug is anything that affects how our body works. Coffee contains caffeine, which can be bad for you if you have too much. Pointy said caffeine is a sort of legal drug. There are other illegal drugs that can do us harm or even kill us.

Alcohol and cigarettes affect the way our bodies work, so Pointy said that they are drugs, too.

Task 1 Which things in these pictures are drugs? Draw a circle around the ones you choose. Abracadada!

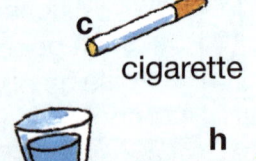

a coke
b sandwich
c cigarette
d oranges
e cake
f aspirin
g water
h cough syrup
i coffee

Task 2 Help me fill in the gaps in these sentences using the words in the box below.

drug   harm   medicines   cigarettes   caffeine

a _____ can make us better when we are sick.

b A _____ is anything that affects how our body works.

c Even coffee contains a sort of drug called _____ which can be bad for you if you have too much.

d There are illegal drugs that can do us _____ or even kill us.

e Alcohol and _____ affect the way our bodies work, so they are drugs, too.

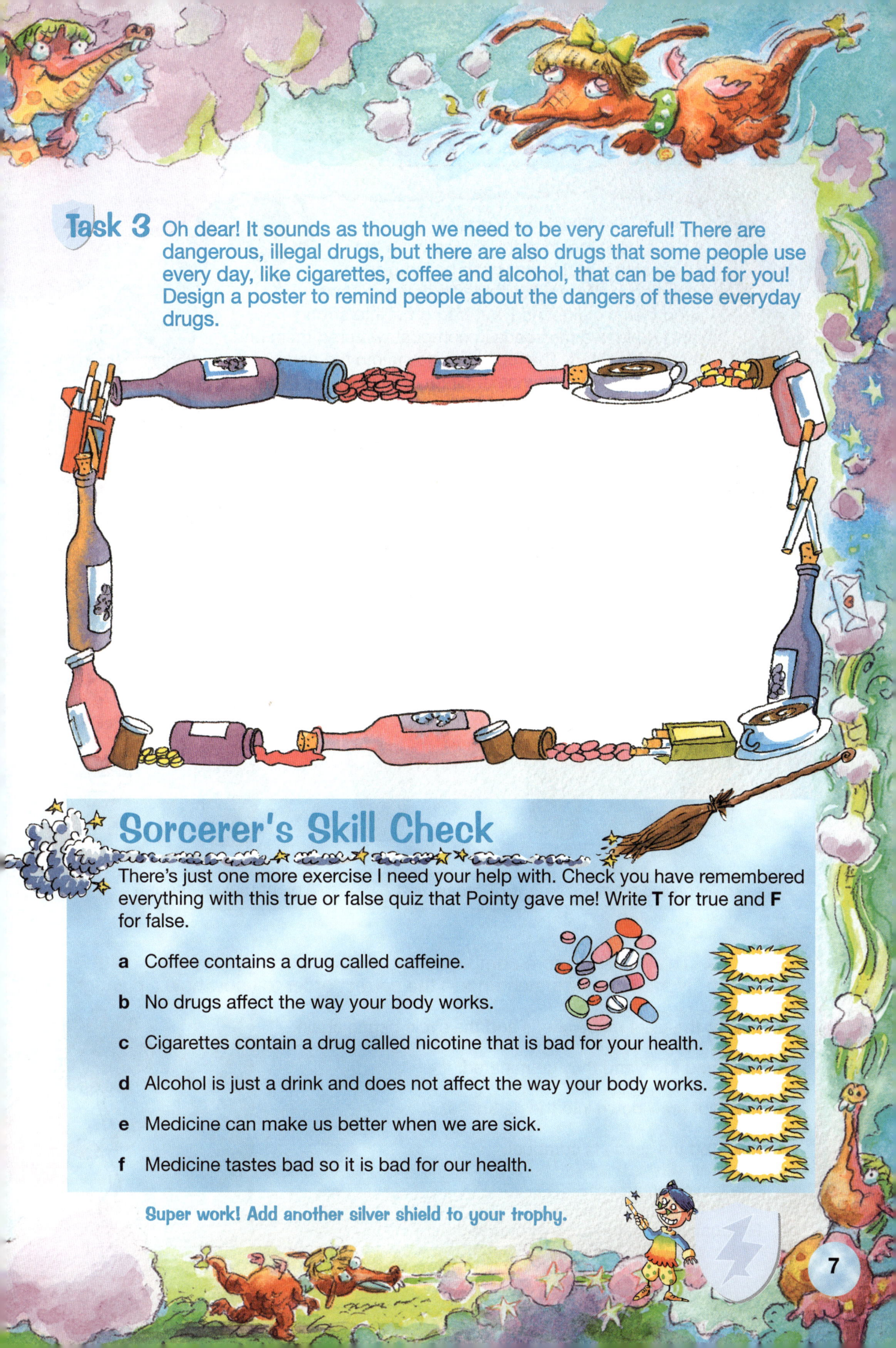

Task 3 Oh dear! It sounds as though we need to be very careful! There are dangerous, illegal drugs, but there are also drugs that some people use every day, like cigarettes, coffee and alcohol, that can be bad for you! Design a poster to remind people about the dangers of these everyday drugs.

Sorcerer's Skill Check

There's just one more exercise I need your help with. Check you have remembered everything with this true or false quiz that Pointy gave me! Write **T** for true and **F** for false.

a Coffee contains a drug called caffeine.

b No drugs affect the way your body works.

c Cigarettes contain a drug called nicotine that is bad for your health.

d Alcohol is just a drink and does not affect the way your body works.

e Medicine can make us better when we are sick.

f Medicine tastes bad so it is bad for our health.

Super work! Add another silver shield to your trophy.

Plant Potions

Pointy here again! I've been looking after the herbs in the greenhouse. They need to be in tip-top condition for Wizard Whimstaff's potions! They need plenty of *light* and *water* to grow into strong plants. I planted the seeds in compost, watered them and they *germinated*. The root grew down into the darkness and the leaves grew next. Gradually the plants grew strong and tall. Super!

Task 1 Work your magic and match the labels to the pictures to describe the lifecycle of a daisy. Join them with a line. Practice makes perfect!

first leaves grow

seed is planted

a  b 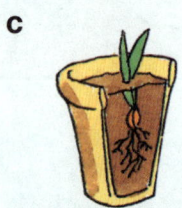 c  d  e

fully grown plant

root grows first

plant makes seeds

Task 2 This is a little more complicated, but you'll soon get the hang of it! Number these statements in the correct order to show how a plant grows.

a Finally, the plant made seeds and the cycle began again.

b I watered them and they germinated.

c The root grew down into the darkness.

d I planted the seeds in compost.

e The leaves grew next.

f Gradually the plants grew strong and tall.

Task 3 Fill in the gaps to make complete sentences, using the words in the boxes below.

leaves   grow   seeds   water   germination   roots   light   temperature

a   When a seed first starts to sprout, we call it _____.

b   Adult plants make _____ and the cycle begins again.

c   _____ grow before the leaves, down into the darkness.

d   After the root has grown down into the soil, the first _____ grow.

e   Plants need _____ to grow tall and strong.

f   Plants need plenty of _____ or they shrivel and go brown.

g   Seeds need water and the correct _____ to germinate.

h   The root always starts to _____ first when a seed germinates.

Sorcerer's Skill Check

Now let's see how much you remember. Can you put these plant lifecycle pictures in the correct order by numbering them below?

a    b    c    d 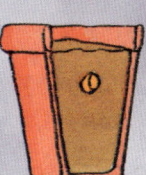   e

Magic yourself another silver shield!

Seed Sorcery

Burp! We're Mugly and Bugly, the lazy frogs! We're always looking inside plants when we're searching for yummy flies. We know about leaves, stems and roots, but what about inside a flower? It's here that seed sorcery takes place! When a plant is pollinated by the wind or an insect, seeds start to form. The seeds make the new plants!

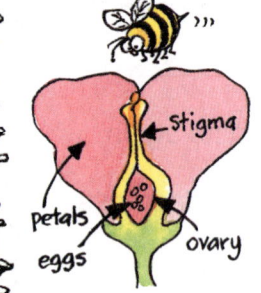

Pollination happens when the pollen from one plant is carried onto the female part of another plant. The pollen travels down a special tube and fertilises the eggs in the ovary of the plant. Plants that are pollinated by the wind have feathery flowers that waft about easily in the wind. Flowers that are pollinated by insects tend to have bright, highly scented flowers.

Yum!

Task 1 Can you match the names of the parts of a plant to the picture while we have a snooze? Write the words in the box below on the diagram, in the labels provided, then wake us up when you've finished.

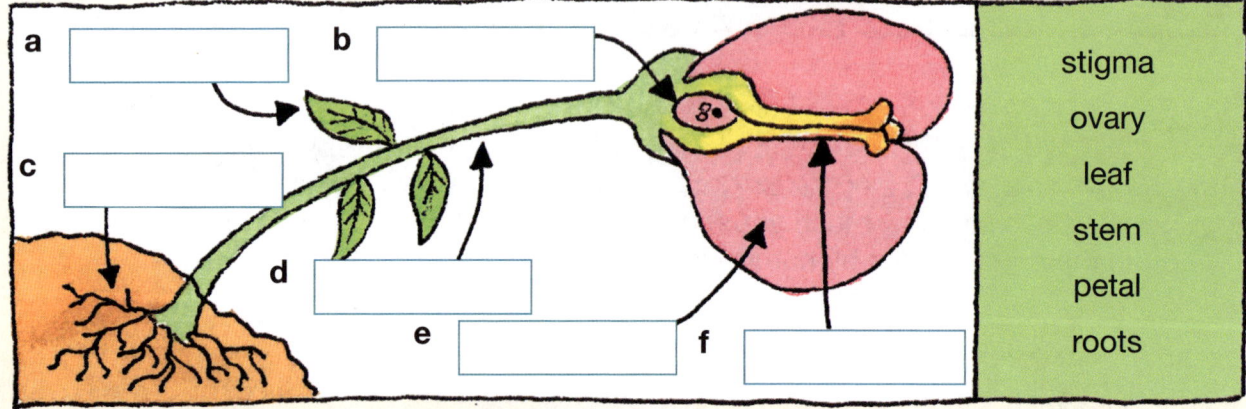

Task 2 Look at the plants below. Do you think they are pollinated by the wind or by an insect? Write **wind** or **insect** in the box. Hurry, grub's up!

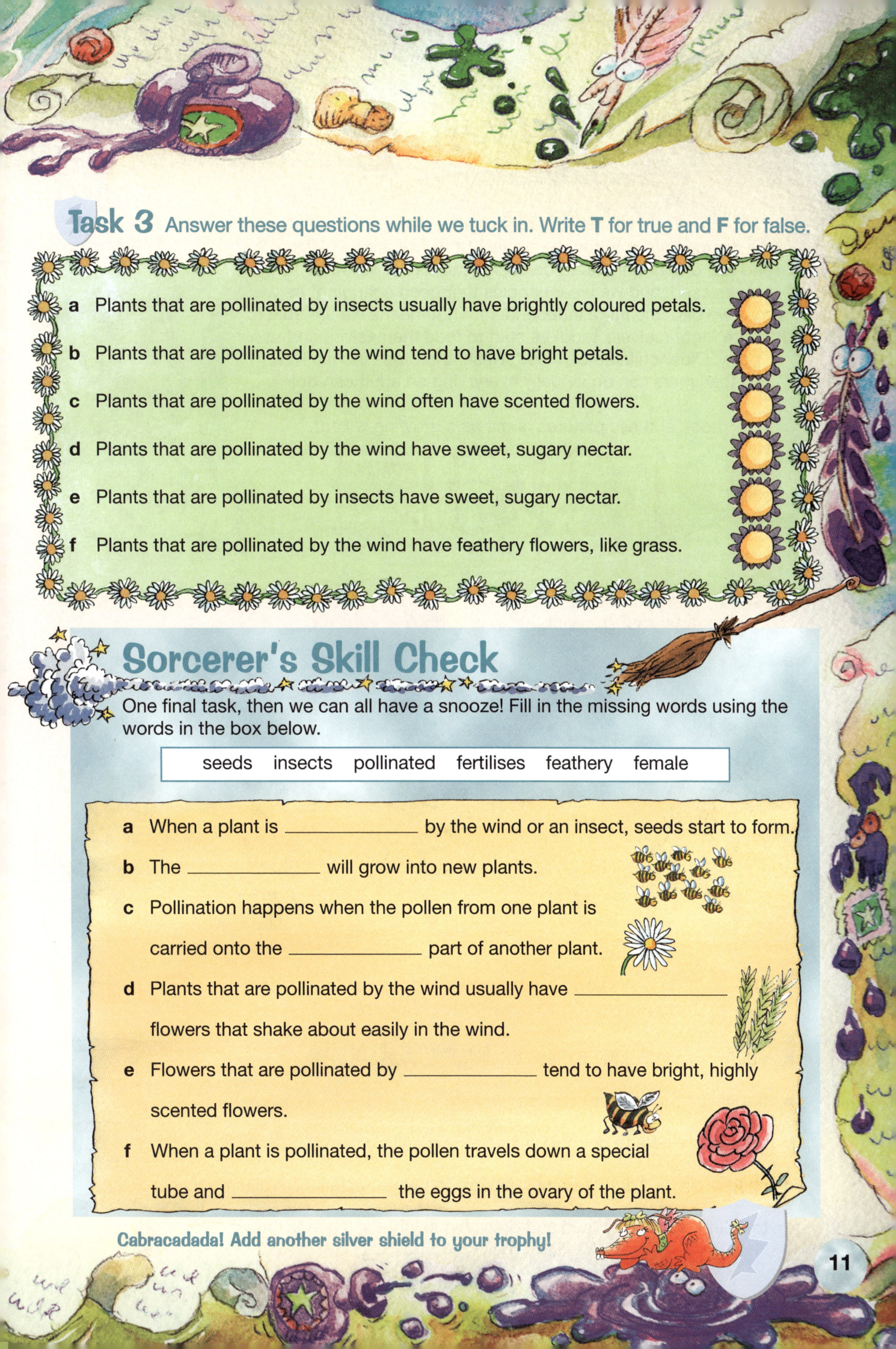

Task 3
Answer these questions while we tuck in. Write **T** for true and **F** for false.

a Plants that are pollinated by insects usually have brightly coloured petals.

b Plants that are pollinated by the wind tend to have bright petals.

c Plants that are pollinated by the wind often have scented flowers.

d Plants that are pollinated by the wind have sweet, sugary nectar.

e Plants that are pollinated by insects have sweet, sugary nectar.

f Plants that are pollinated by the wind have feathery flowers, like grass.

Sorcerer's Skill Check

One final task, then we can all have a snooze! Fill in the missing words using the words in the box below.

> seeds   insects   pollinated   fertilises   feathery   female

a When a plant is _____ by the wind or an insect, seeds start to form.

b The _____ will grow into new plants.

c Pollination happens when the pollen from one plant is carried onto the _____ part of another plant.

d Plants that are pollinated by the wind usually have _____ flowers that shake about easily in the wind.

e Flowers that are pollinated by _____ tend to have bright, highly scented flowers.

f When a plant is pollinated, the pollen travels down a special tube and _____ the eggs in the ovary of the plant.

Cabracadada! Add another silver shield to your trophy!

Grisly Growing

Humans change a great deal as they **grow**. When we are first born, we are helpless and rely on our parents to do everything for us. We need to be fed, dressed, and we wear nappies that need changing! As we grow, we become more independent. That means we are able to do more for ourselves. Toddlers start to feed themselves and use a potty. Older children can feed, wash and dress themselves. Teenagers can do virtually everything an adult can do!

Look at these pictures of me as a growing wizard.

Task 1 Can you put these pictures of Pointy in order, from a baby goblin to the fine young assistant he is today?

a   b   c   d   e

Task 2 Excellent work! Now, number these sentences describing me in order from babyhood to adulthood. Allakazan!

a **adult** – can look after himself totally!

b **baby** – unable to feed or dress himself.

c **teenager** – able to do most things for himself.

d **child** – can feed and dress but not able to take complete care of himself.

e **toddler** – starting to feed and dress himself but still needs lots of help.

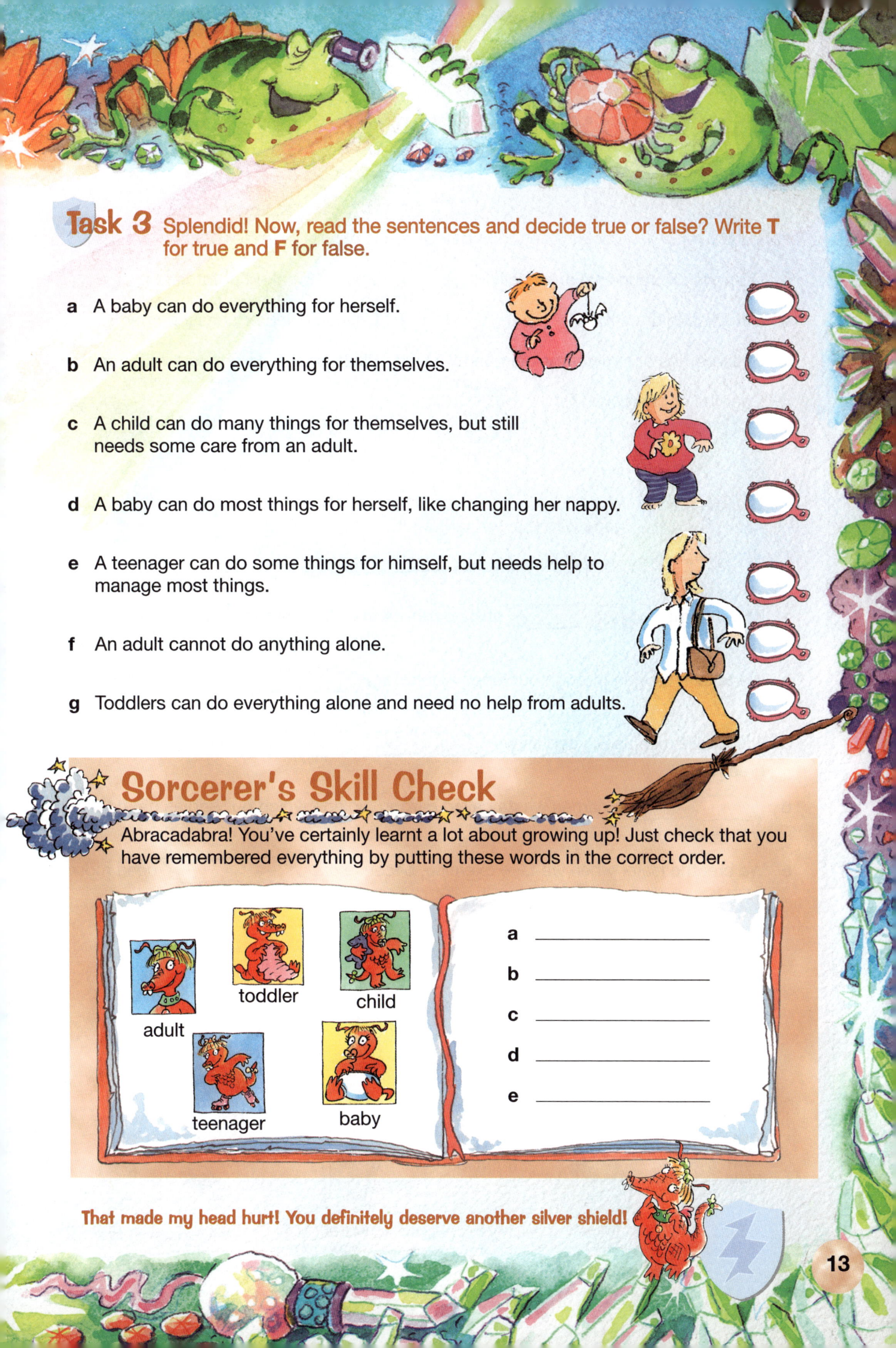

Task 3
Splendid! Now, read the sentences and decide true or false? Write **T** for true and **F** for false.

a A baby can do everything for herself.

b An adult can do everything for themselves.

c A child can do many things for themselves, but still needs some care from an adult.

d A baby can do most things for herself, like changing her nappy.

e A teenager can do some things for himself, but needs help to manage most things.

f An adult cannot do anything alone.

g Toddlers can do everything alone and need no help from adults.

Sorcerer's Skill Check

Abracadabra! You've certainly learnt a lot about growing up! Just check that you have remembered everything by putting these words in the correct order.

adult   toddler   child   teenager   baby

a _____
b _____
c _____
d _____
e _____

That made my head hurt! You definitely deserve another silver shield!

Apprentice Wizard Challenge 1

Challenge 1 Look at the foods below and circle the healthier option.

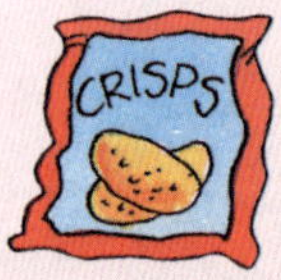
CRISPS

a Oranges or orange flavoured jelly?

b Carrot cake or carrots?

c Strawberries or strawberry ice cream?

d Cherries or cherry jam?

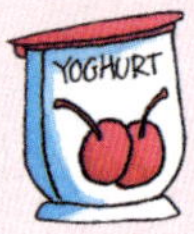
YOGHURT

e Crisps or baked potatoes?

f Cheese salad or cheeseburger?

g Pizza and chips or pasta with tomato sauce?

h Oranges or marmalade?

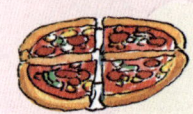

Challenge 2 What do you know about blood? Answer the questions, filling the gaps with the words from the box below.

breathe muscles oxygen exercise blood

a Blood carries ________ and goodness from food around our bodies.

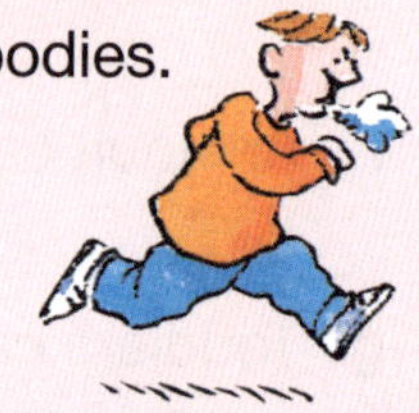

b We take in oxygen through our lungs when we ________.

c Our bodies use up oxygen as we ________. That is why we become breathless.

d ________ carries waste called carbon dioxide which our bodies get rid of as we breathe out.

e We breathe faster when we take exercise, because our ________ need more oxygen.

Challenge 3 Which things in these pictures are not drugs? Draw a circle around the ones you choose.

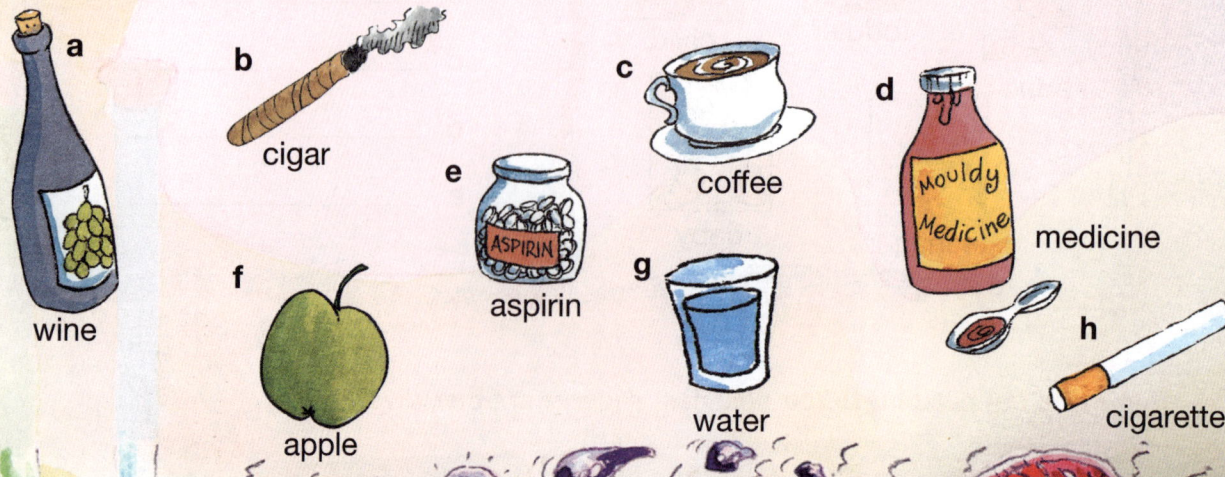

a
wine
b
cigar
c
coffee
d
Mouldy Medicine
medicine
e
ASPIRIN
aspirin
f
apple
g
water
h
cigarette

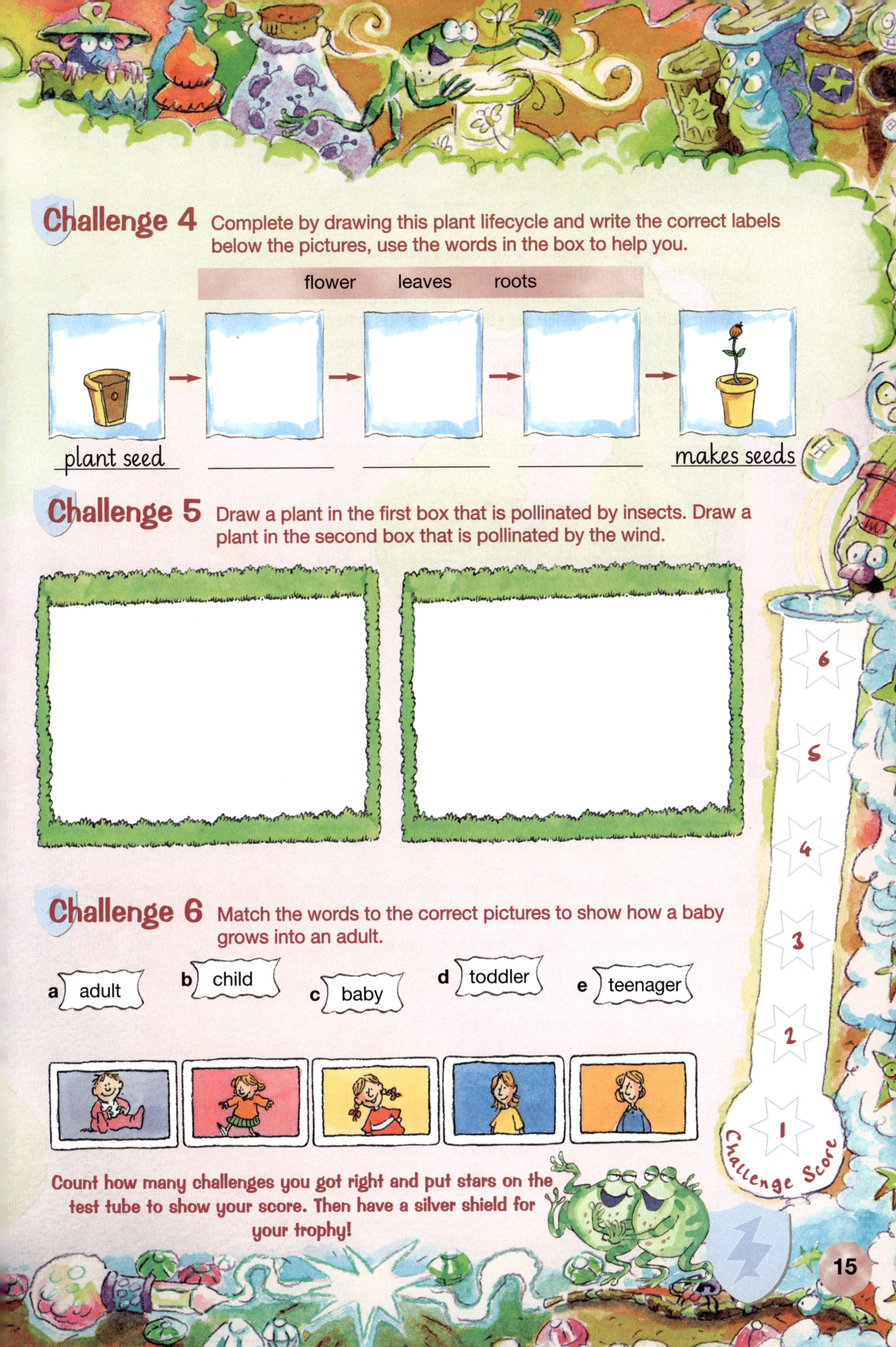

Mucky Micro Organisms

Micro organism is the name given to very small living things, such as a virus, bacteria or fungus. I find micro organisms very confusing! Wizard Whimstaff says they can be very dangerous and make people (and dragons!) poorly, but they can also be useful! I love bread and Pointy told me it is made using a micro organism called yeast. He said yoghurt is made with a micro organism too!

Task 1 My head hurts with all this thinking! Help me by filling in the missing words.

| yoghurt   micro organism   mouldy   germs   ill   viruses   bacteria |

a Bread is made using a _____.

b Micro organisms are added to milk to make _____.

c The _____ that gives us upset tummies is a micro organism.

d Colds and 'flu are caused by _____.

e The green stuff that grows on _____ bread is a micro organism.

f You should always wash your hands before cooking in case you have _____ or bacteria on your hands.

g Viruses and bacteria are both micro organisms that can make you _____.

16

Task 2 This is more difficult. Can you tell me if these statements are true **T** or false **F**?

a Yoghurt is made using a micro organism.

b Bacteria is a type of micro organism.

c Viruses are not micro organisms.

d You should never wash your hands before cooking to make sure you have bacteria on your hands.

e The mould on bread is a type of micro organism.

Task 3 Can you match the correct beginnings and endings, by drawing a line between the sentences?

a Colds	to wash away bacteria and viruses.
b We cover our mouths when we cough	to keep flies away. They carry micro organisms that can make us sick.
c We cover food	so we don't spread viruses to other people.
d We wash our hands before we handle food	to keep it cool. Bacteria finds it easier to grow in warm places.
e We keep perishable food in the fridge	are caused by a virus.

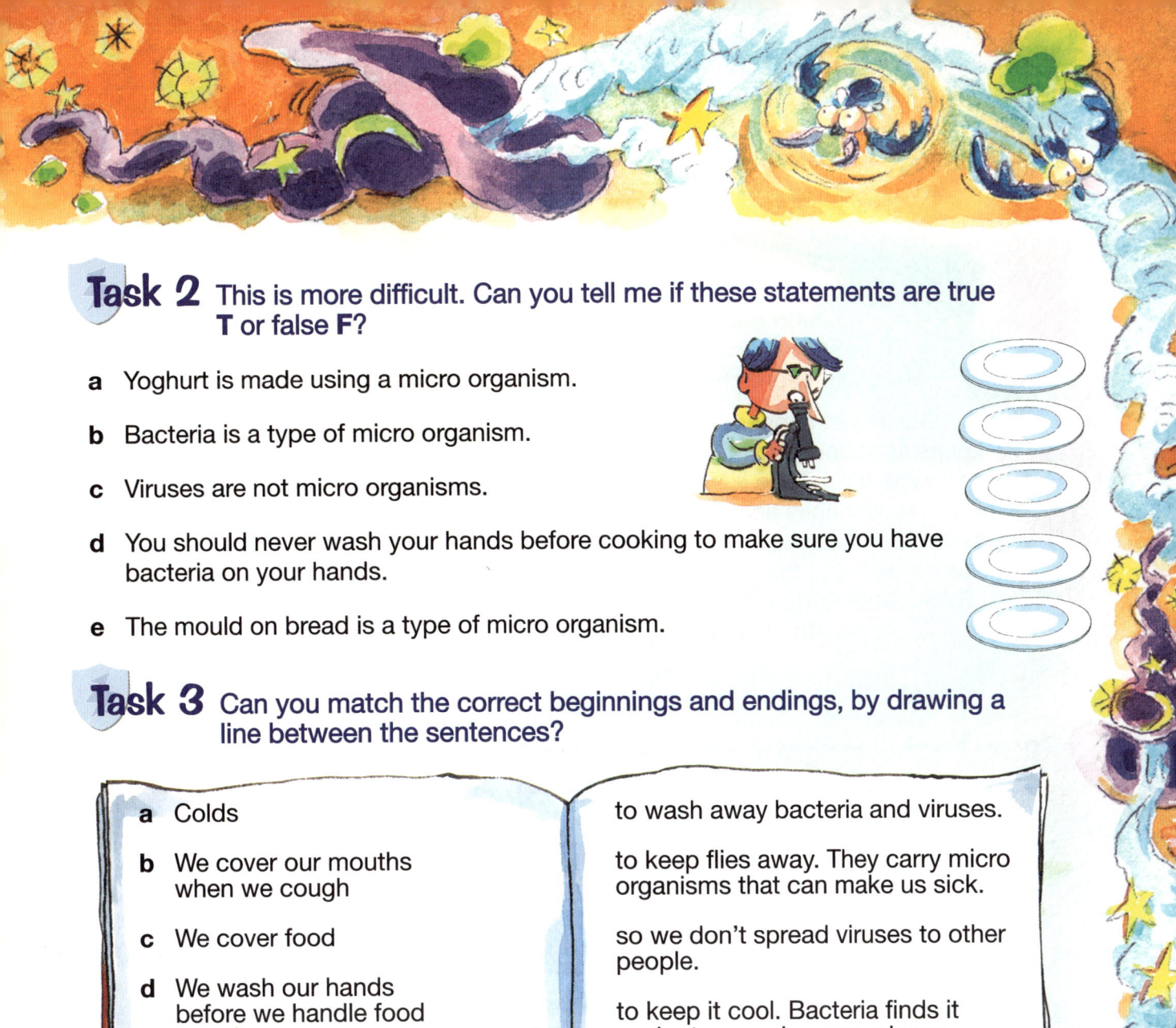

Sorcerer's Skill Check

Just to check that you have remembered the things you need to know, write a list of rules for keeping safe around the harmful type of micro organisms.

a _____

b _____

c _____

d _____

Abracadabra! You deserve another silver shield for your trophy!

Gruesome Gases

Have you ever thought about the gases we use every day? There's air, of course – without that most useful gas, we couldn't breathe! Air contains oxygen, another gas.

Gas is a strange thing. It's not like a solid, which generally keeps its shape, and takes up the same amount of space. It's not like a liquid either, which takes on different shapes according to the container it is in, but also takes up the same amount of space. Gas spreads out to fill whatever space it is given. Think about how smoke spreads out and you'll soon get the hang of it!

Task 1 Spot the gas! Look at the picture below. Apart from the air that fills the room, where can you see gas in the picture below? Draw around each example.

Task 2 Super! Fill in the gaps in the sentences, using the words from the box below. It's easy when you know how!

fill   breathe   gas   oxygen   fizzy   air

a _____ is a gas found all around us. This is the gas we breathe!

b Gas spreads out to _____ any space where it is released.

c Air contains _____, which is another gas!

d Some people have _____ powered cookers.

e When you drink a _____ drink, the gas is what makes it fizz!

f Without air, we would not be able to _____.

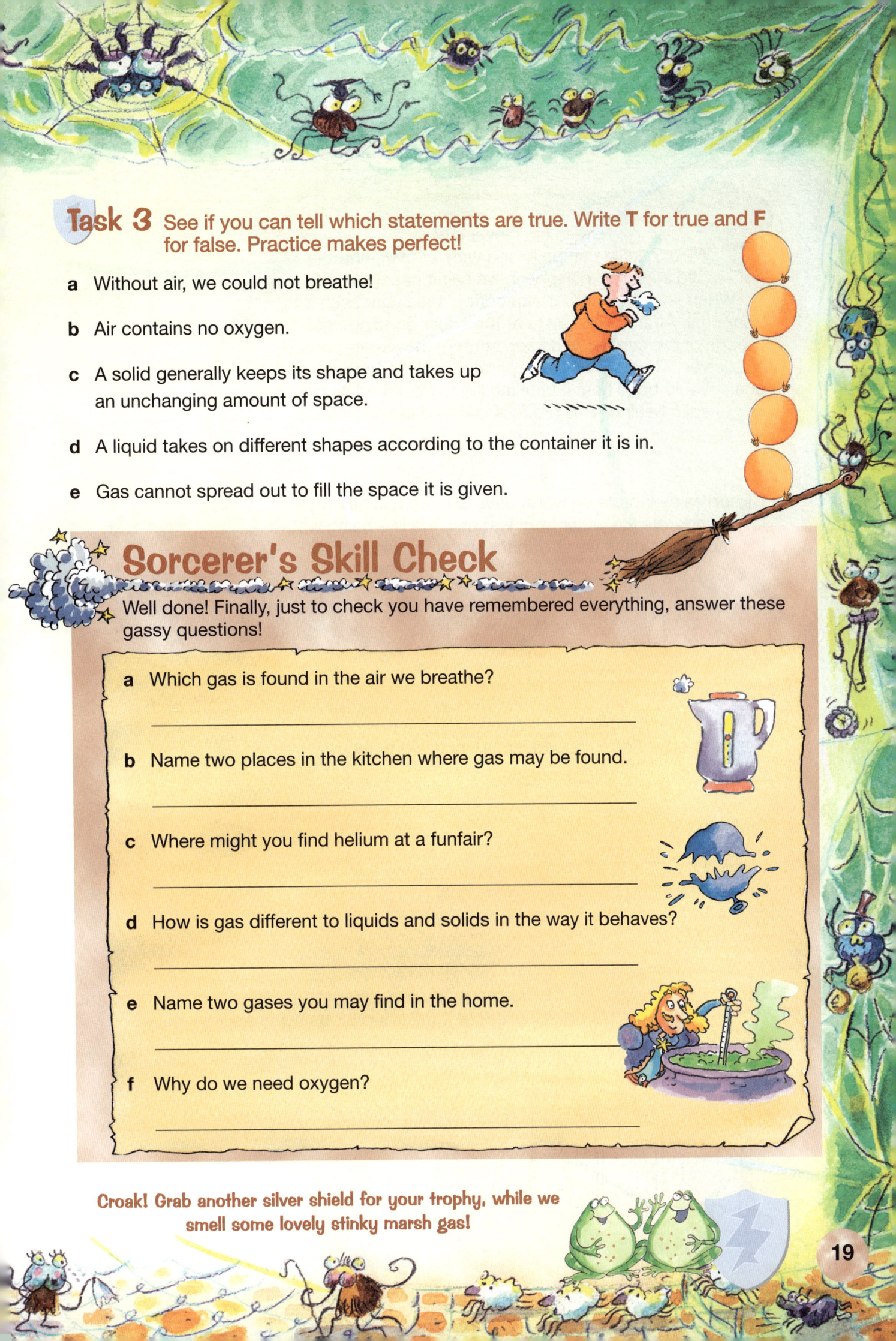

Task 3 See if you can tell which statements are true. Write **T** for true and **F** for false. Practice makes perfect!

a Without air, we could not breathe!

b Air contains no oxygen.

c A solid generally keeps its shape and takes up an unchanging amount of space.

d A liquid takes on different shapes according to the container it is in.

e Gas cannot spread out to fill the space it is given.

Sorcerer's Skill Check

Well done! Finally, just to check you have remembered everything, answer these gassy questions!

a Which gas is found in the air we breathe?
_____

b Name two places in the kitchen where gas may be found.
_____

c Where might you find helium at a funfair?
_____

d How is gas different to liquids and solids in the way it behaves?
_____

e Name two gases you may find in the home.
_____

f Why do we need oxygen?
_____

Croak! Grab another silver shield for your trophy, while we smell some lovely stinky marsh gas!

Dissolving and Evaporating

Listen up, clever clogs!
When a **solid** can be mixed with a **liquid**, and the solid seems to disappear, we say it has **dissolved**. When you add sugar to hot coffee, the sugar seems to disappear. At first, you can hear the sugar grinding against the edge of the cup. As you keep stirring, the sugar gradually dissolves. The only way to separate the solid from the liquid again would be to heat it until the liquid boiled off, leaving the solid behind. This process is called **evaporation**.

Puddles evaporate on warm days and we use hair dryers to evaporate the water from wet hair. We like being wet, so on hot days we stay in the water, to keep moist!

Task 1 Croak! Which of these involve evaporation? Put a tick (✔) on the lily pad.

a Cleaning leaves out of a paddling pool using a net.

b Separating salt from sea water to make fresh water.

c Draining the water from a pan of potatoes for dinner.

d Leaving a dish of salty water on the windowsill so the water dries in the sun and makes crystals.

e Blow-drying your hair.

Task 2 Brain cell alert! Using the following equipment, draw a diagram to show how you would separate salt from water, using evaporation.

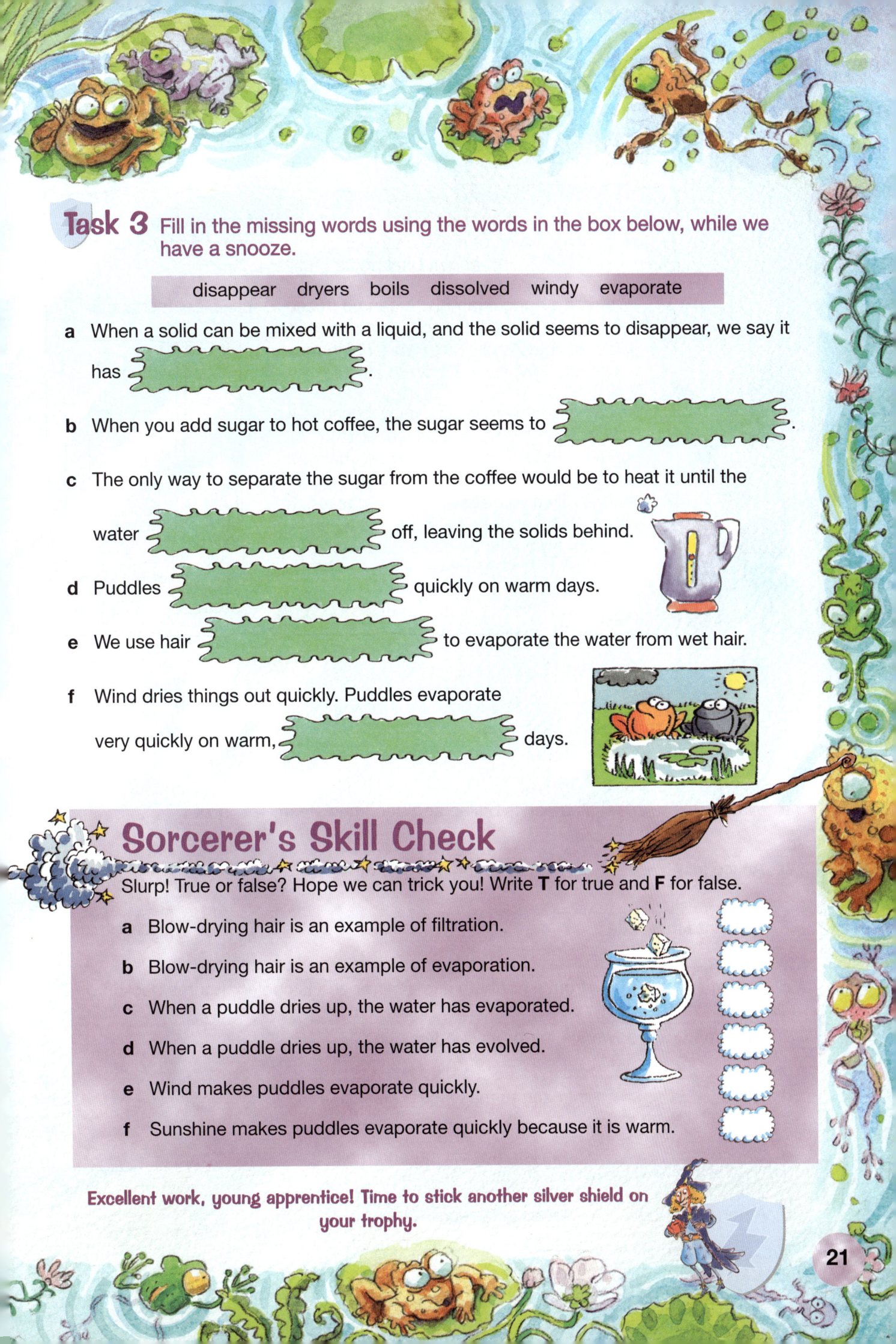

Task 3 Fill in the missing words using the words in the box below, while we have a snooze.

> disappear   dryers   boils   dissolved   windy   evaporate

a When a solid can be mixed with a liquid, and the solid seems to disappear, we say it has _____.

b When you add sugar to hot coffee, the sugar seems to _____.

c The only way to separate the sugar from the coffee would be to heat it until the water _____ off, leaving the solids behind.

d Puddles _____ quickly on warm days.

e We use hair _____ to evaporate the water from wet hair.

f Wind dries things out quickly. Puddles evaporate very quickly on warm, _____ days.

Sorcerer's Skill Check

Slurp! True or false? Hope we can trick you! Write **T** for true and **F** for false.

a Blow-drying hair is an example of filtration.

b Blow-drying hair is an example of evaporation.

c When a puddle dries up, the water has evaporated.

d When a puddle dries up, the water has evolved.

e Wind makes puddles evaporate quickly.

f Sunshine makes puddles evaporate quickly because it is warm.

Excellent work, young apprentice! Time to stick another silver shield on your trophy.

Spooky States

We can **change the state** (solid, liquid or gas) of materials by heating and cooling. Some of these changes can be **reversed** and the material changed back to its **original state**.

Water is a good example. It can be frozen to make ice. It changes from a liquid to a solid. And ice can be melted again, changing back into water, which means it changes from a solid to a liquid.

We call this a **reversible change**, because we have changed the material back into its original state. Water can also be changed from a liquid to a gas (steam) by heating. This change can also be reversed, by cooling the steam. Think about what happens when hot steam from a kettle hits a cold kitchen window.

You'll soon get the hang of it!

Task 1

Water can be changed from one state (solid, liquid, gas) to another. Fill in the blanks below to show what state the water is in at each stage. Super!

a Water ⟨ liquid ⟩ in a pan is boiled and becomes steam ⟨ gas ⟩.

b An ice lolly ⟨ ⟩ melts in the sun and turns back into fruit juice ⟨ ⟩.

c Steam ⟨ ⟩ from a hot bath hits a mirror and is cooled. It turns back into water and runs down the mirror as condensation ⟨ ⟩.

d Water ⟨ ⟩ is frozen to make ice cubes ⟨ ⟩.

e Chocolate ⟨ ⟩ is left in a hot car and melts ⟨ ⟩.

f A pond ⟨ ⟩ freezes and becomes ice ⟨ ⟩.

Task 2 Now look at these sentences and work your magic to fill in the gaps, using the words in the box below.

> gas   reversible   state   liquid   solid

a   We can change the _____ of materials by heating and cooling.

b   Some of these changes can be reversed and the material changed back to its original state. We call this a _____ change.

c   When water is frozen, it changes from a _____ to a solid.

d   When ice is melted, it changes from a _____ to a liquid.

e   Water can also be changed from a liquid to a _____ by boiling it.

Task 3 Look at these statements. Are they true **T** or false **F**? It's easy when you know how!

a   Water can be changed from a liquid to a gas (steam) by heating.

b   When steam is cooled it turns into a gas.

c   When water is frozen, it turns into steam.

d   When water is frozen, it turns into ice.

e   When steam hits a cold surface, it cools down and turns into water.

Sorcerer's Skill Check

Practice makes perfect! Look at the pictures and write **solid**, **liquid** or **gas** underneath each one.

a   b   c   d   e

Croak! Watching you has worn us out! Grab another silver shield while we grab forty winks!

Powerful Planets

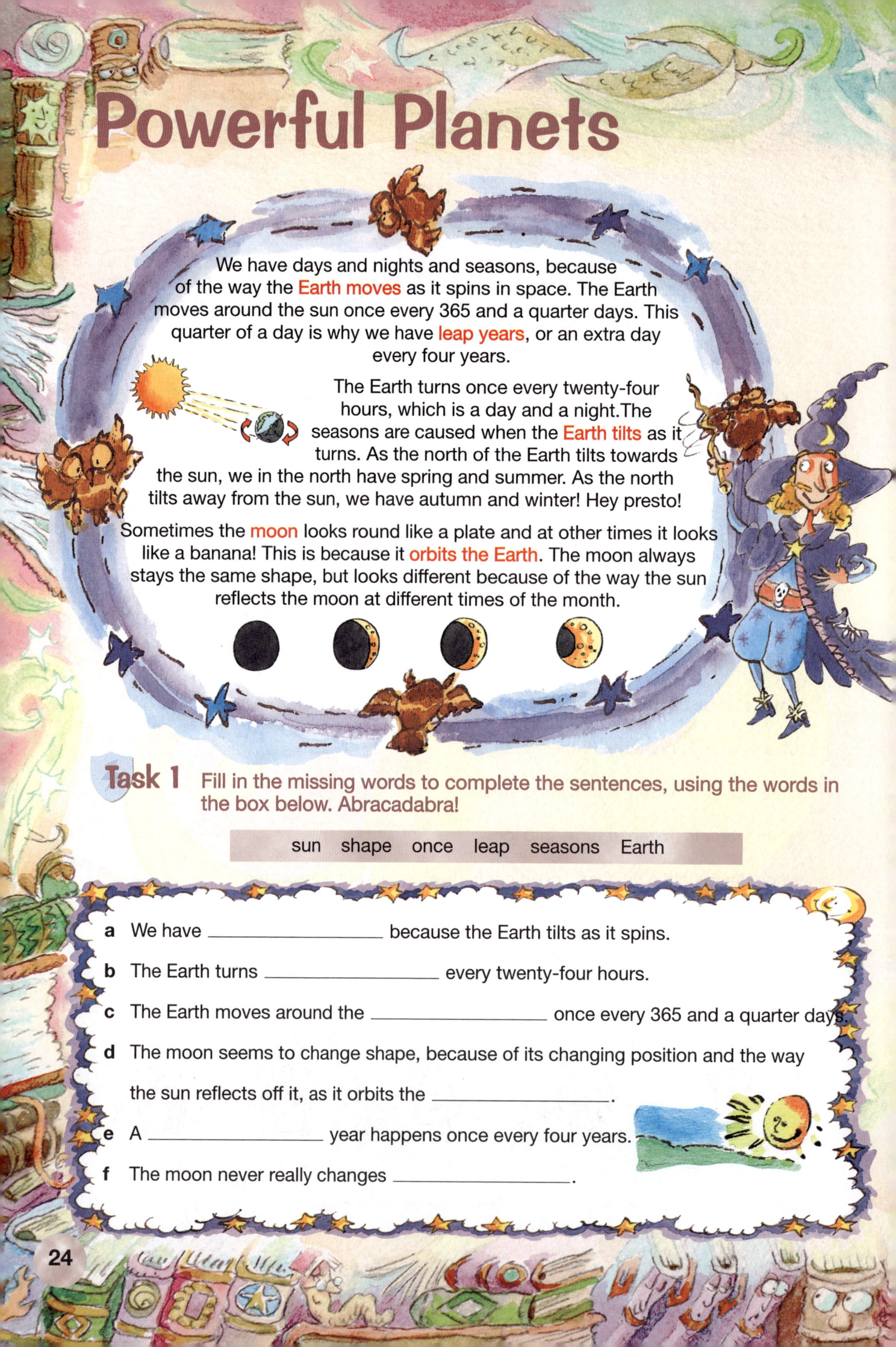

We have days and nights and seasons, because of the way the Earth moves as it spins in space. The Earth moves around the sun once every 365 and a quarter days. This quarter of a day is why we have leap years, or an extra day every four years.

The Earth turns once every twenty-four hours, which is a day and a night. The seasons are caused when the Earth tilts as it turns. As the north of the Earth tilts towards the sun, we in the north have spring and summer. As the north tilts away from the sun, we have autumn and winter! Hey presto!

Sometimes the moon looks round like a plate and at other times it looks like a banana! This is because it orbits the Earth. The moon always stays the same shape, but looks different because of the way the sun reflects the moon at different times of the month.

Task 1 Fill in the missing words to complete the sentences, using the words in the box below. Abracadabra!

> sun   shape   once   leap   seasons   Earth

a   We have _____ because the Earth tilts as it spins.

b   The Earth turns _____ every twenty-four hours.

c   The Earth moves around the _____ once every 365 and a quarter days.

d   The moon seems to change shape, because of its changing position and the way the sun reflects off it, as it orbits the _____.

e   A _____ year happens once every four years.

f   The moon never really changes _____.

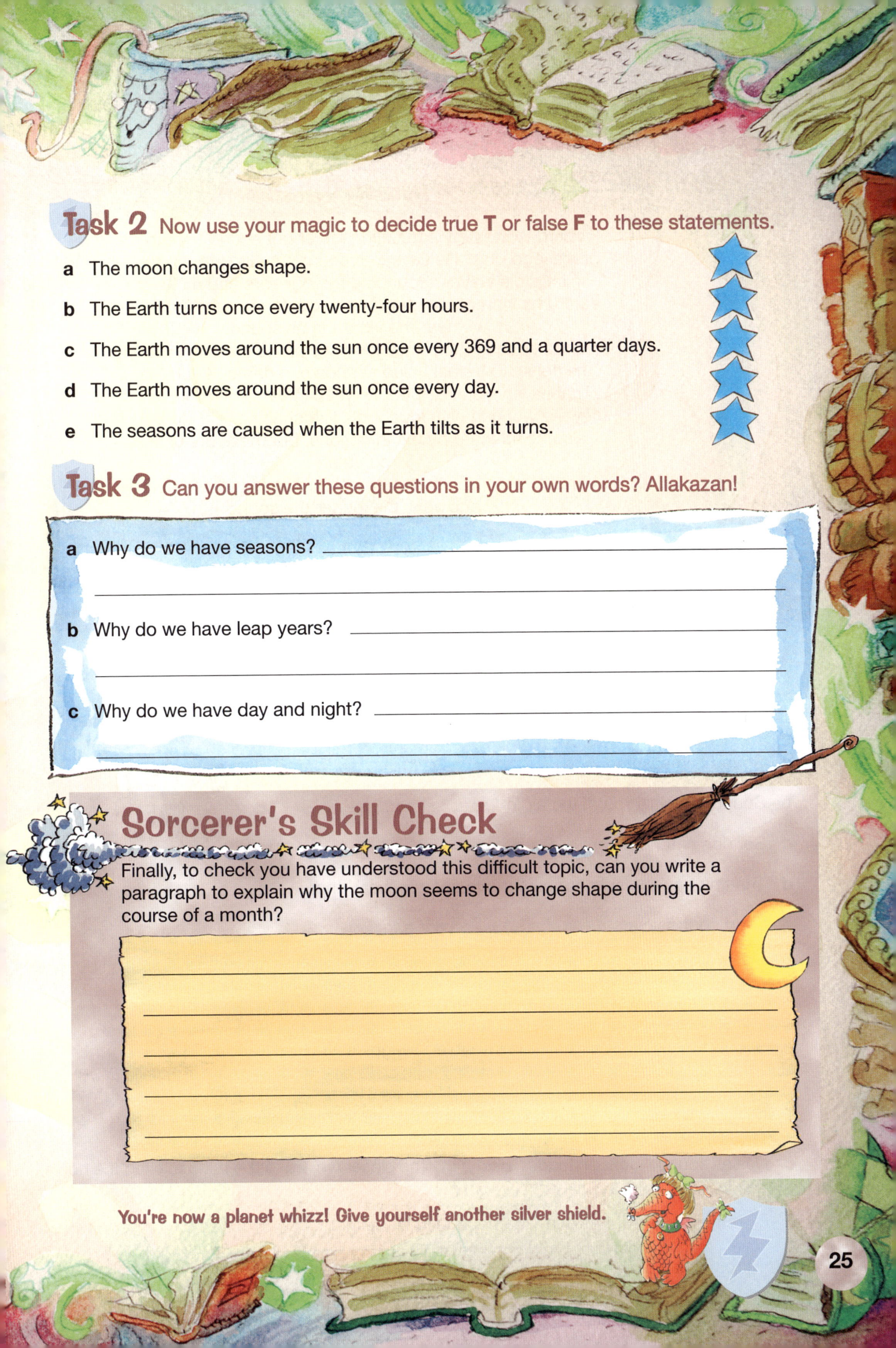

Task 2 Now use your magic to decide true **T** or false **F** to these statements.

a The moon changes shape.

b The Earth turns once every twenty-four hours.

c The Earth moves around the sun once every 369 and a quarter days.

d The Earth moves around the sun once every day.

e The seasons are caused when the Earth tilts as it turns.

Task 3 Can you answer these questions in your own words? Allakazan!

a Why do we have seasons? _____

b Why do we have leap years? _____

c Why do we have day and night? _____

Sorcerer's Skill Check

Finally, to check you have understood this difficult topic, can you write a paragraph to explain why the moon seems to change shape during the course of a month?

You're now a planet whizz! Give yourself another silver shield.

Sensational Sounds

Wizard Whimstaff is teaching me about sound to help me practise roaring. He says that sound travels through the air in invisible waves. Sounds enter our ears and make our eardrums vibrate. The tiny bones inside our ears move and we hear the vibration as sound.
Noises sound louder the closer we are to the thing making the noise. Extremely loud sounds can damage your ears. That is why you see people wearing ear protectors when they are working with loud tools like chainsaws. Hearing can also be affected by ear infections, but these are usually curable.
Sound is measured in decibels (dB). The higher the number of decibels, the louder the sound.

Task 1
Help me to roar loudly by filling in the missing words to complete the sentences.

waves   vibration   decibels   damage   eardrums

a Sound is measured in _____ (dB).

b Sound travels through the air in _____.

c Sounds enter our ears and make our _____ vibrate.

d The tiny bones inside our ears move and we 'hear' the _____ as 'sound'.

e Loud sounds can _____ your ears.

Task 2
Can you choose the correct word so that the sentences make sense? Cross out the wrong words so I don't get confused.

a Sound travels through the air in invisible   wiggles waves wands

b Sounds enter our ears and make our   ears eggs eardrums   vibrate.

c Noises sound   louder longer best   the closer we are to the thing making the noise.

d Extremely loud sounds can   damage excite delight   your ears.

Task 3
Look at the picture below. Circle where the dragon sounds the loudest, **A**, **B** or **C**.

Where would the dragon sound the quietest? Give a reason for your answer

_____
_____

Sorcerer's Skill Check

These are very difficult! Write **T** for true and **F** for false.

a Sound moves in straight lines through the air.

b We hear things as sound enters our ears and makes our eardrums vibrate.

c People wear earmuffs to protect their ears by muffling loud noises.

d We hear things as sound enters our noses and makes the nose hairs vibrate.

e Soft noises can damage the ears.

f Loud noises can damage hearing. That's why people wear ear protectors when they operate heavy machinery.

You soon got the hang of sound! Time for another silver shield!

Apprentice Wizard Challenge 2

Challenge 1 Design a poster to tell people the difference between harmful and helpful micro organisms in the kitchen.

Challenge 2 Which statements about solids, liquids and gases are true? Write **T** for true and **F** for false.

a We need oxygen to be able to breathe.

b Air is made up mostly from helium, like in balloons.

c A liquid generally keeps its shape and takes up the same amount of space.

d A solid takes on different shapes according to the container it is in.

e Solids spread out to fill whatever space they are given.

f Gas spreads out to fill the space it is given.

Challenge 3 Draw a diagram on the parchment below to show how you would separate sugar from water, using evaporation. Write a list of the equipment you would need:

Diagram   Equipment

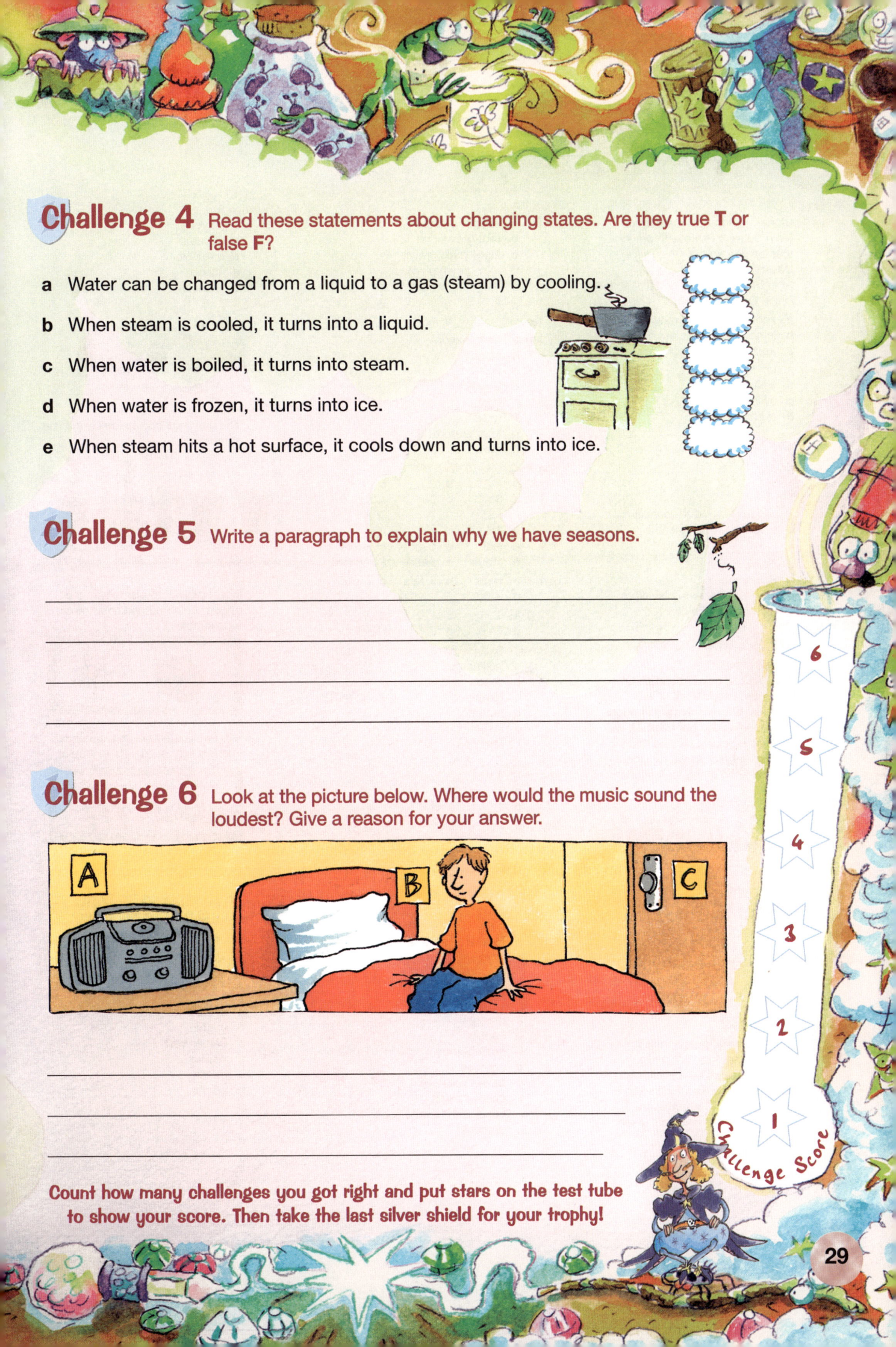

Challenge 4 Read these statements about changing states. Are they true **T** or false **F**?

a Water can be changed from a liquid to a gas (steam) by cooling.
b When steam is cooled, it turns into a liquid.
c When water is boiled, it turns into steam.
d When water is frozen, it turns into ice.
e When steam hits a hot surface, it cools down and turns into ice.

Challenge 5 Write a paragraph to explain why we have seasons.

_____
_____
_____
_____

Challenge 6 Look at the picture below. Where would the music sound the loudest? Give a reason for your answer.

_____
_____
_____

Count how many challenges you got right and put stars on the test tube to show your score. Then take the last silver shield for your trophy!

Answers

Pages 2–3

Task 1 Starter: Melon with raspberries
Main Course: Pasta with dragon-roasted vegetables
Dessert: Fruit Salad
After Dinner: Grapes and fruit sorbet
Drink: Orange juice

Task 2
- a cherries
- b lemons
- c apples
- d oranges
- e blackberries
- f potatoes

Task 3
- a go jogging
- b walking briskly
- c swimming
- d cycling

Sorcerer's Skill Check
- a F   b T   c T
- d F   e F

Pages 4–5

Task 1
- a oxygen
- b muscles
- c blood
- d dissolved
- e breathe
- f lungs

Task 2
- a Pointy cycling
- b Pointy running
- c Miss Snufflebeam playing football with Pointy

Task 3
- a T   b F   c T
- d T   e F

Sorcerer's Skill Check
Exercise makes our hearts beat faster and keeps us fit. If we exercise, our muscles get stronger and that includes our hearts! If we exercise regularly, we find that we get less 'puffed' as we run about – and can keep going for longer!

Pages 6–7

Task 1

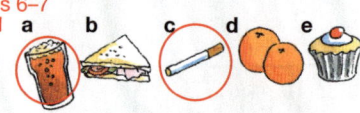

Task 2
- a medicines
- b drug
- c caffeine
- d harm
- e cigarettes

Task 3 Any poster that puts across the following message is correct: Everyday drugs, like caffeine and alcohol, can be harmful if taken in large amounts. Cigarettes are harmful however many are taken.

Sorcerer's Skill Check
- a T   b F   c T
- d F   e T   f F

Pages 8–9

Task 1
- a seed is planted
- b root grows first
- c first leaves grow
- d fully grown plant
- e plant makes seeds

Task 2
- a 6   b 2   c 3
- d 1   e 4   f 5

Task 3
- a germination
- b seeds
- c roots
- d leaves
- e light
- f water
- g temperature
- h grow

Sorcerer's Skill Check
- a 4   b 2   c 1
- d 3   e 5

Pages 10–11

Task 1
- a leaf   b ovary   c roots
- d stem   e petal   f stigma

Task 2
- a wind   b insect   c insect
- d wind

Task 3
- a T   b F   c F
- d F   e T   f T

Sorcerer's Skill Check
- a pollinated
- b seeds
- c female
- d feathery
- e insects
- f fertilises

Pages 12–13

Task 1
- a 3   b 5   c 2
- d 1   e 4

Task 2
- a 5   b 1   c 4
- d 3   e 2

Task 3
- a F   d F   f F
- b T   e F   g F
- c T

Sorcerer's Skill Check
- a baby   d teenager
- b toddler   e adult
- c child

Pages 14–15

Challenge 1
- a oranges
- b carrots
- c strawberries
- d cherries
- e baked potatoes
- f cheese salad
- g pasta with tomato sauce
- h oranges

Challenge 2
- a oxygen
- b breathe
- c exercise
- d blood
- e muscles

Challenge 3

Challenge 4
The drawings should look like these samples:

plant seed   roots   leaves   flower   makes seeds

Challenge 5
Insect pollinated plants would be brightly coloured and smell sweet, for example:

Wind pollinated plants would have feathery light seeds, for example:

Challenge 6

Pages 16–17

Task 1
- a micro organism
- b yoghurt
- c bacteria
- d viruses
- e mouldy
- f germs
- g ill

Task 2
- a T   b T   c F
- d F   e T

Task 3
a Colds are caused by a virus.
b We cover our mouths when we cough so we don't spread viruses to other people.
c We cover food to keep flies away. They carry micro organisms that can make us sick.
d We wash our hands before we handle food to wash away bacteria and viruses.
e We keep perishable food in the fridge to keep it cool. Bacteria finds it easier to grow in warm places.

Sorcerer's Skill Check
Suggested answers are:
a Wash your hands before handling food.
b Cover your mouth when you cough or sneeze.
c Wash your hands after using the toilet.
d Never eat mouldy food.

Pages 18–19
Task 1

Task 2
a air   d gas
b fill   e fizzy
c oxygen   f breathe

Task 3
a T   b F   c T
d T   e F

Sorcerer's Skill Check
Answers may include:
a oxygen
b steam coming out of kettle, gas cooker and fizzy drink.
c In balloons.
d Gas spreads out to fill the space, liquid takes on the shape of the container it is in, or but takes up the same space.
e oxygen, air or natural gas
f To breathe and make our muscles work.

Pages 20–21
Task 1 b, d and e all involve evaporation.
Task 2 The diagram should show beaker placed over heat to evaporate water.
Task 3
a dissolved
b disappear
c boils
d evaporate
e dryers
f windy

Sorcerer's Skill Check
a F   b T   c T
d F   e T   f T

Pages 22–23
Task 1
a liquid and gas
b solid and liquid
c gas and liquid
d liquid and solid
e solid and liquid
f liquid and solid

Task 2
a state
b reversible
c liquid
d solid
e gas

Task 3
a T   b F   c F
d T   e T

Sorcerer's Skill Check
a gas   b liquid   c solid
d gas   e solid

Pages 24–25
Task 1
a seasons   d Earth
b once   e leap
c sun   f shape

Task 2
a F   b T   c F
d F   e T

Task 3
a We have seasons because the Earth tilts as it turns.
b We have leap years because the Earth takes 365 and a quarter days to orbit the sun.
c We have day and night because the Earth turns, and so only certain parts face the sun.

Sorcerer's Skill Check
The moon appears to change shape because sunlight reflects off the moon differently at different times of the month.

Pages 26–27
Task 1
a decibels
b waves
c eardrums
d vibration
e damage

Task 2
a waves
b eardrums
c louder
d damage

Task 3 The dragon would sound the loudest at the position closest to it (A). This is because the closer you are to the thing that made the sound, the louder the noise. The dragon would sound the quietest at (C), because the further you are from the thing making the noise, the quieter it sounds, as the sound has further to travel.

Sorcerer's Skill Check
a F   b T   c T
d F   e F   f T

Pages 28–29
Challenge 1
Any poster is correct that explains how some micro organisms are harmful and are killed by cleaning chemicals or high temperatures, but also that micro-organisms can be used to make great things (beer, yoghurt and bread).

Challenge 2
a T   b F   c F
d F   e F   f T

Challenge 3
Any diagram explaining how the water would be placed over heat to evaporate water to get sugar, and a list of equipment (beaker, sugary water and heat source).

Challenge 4
a F   b T   c T
d T   e F

Challenge 5
An example answer would be: We have seasons because the Earth tilts as it rotates. As the Earth tilts towards the sun, we in the north have spring and summer. As the Earth tiltes away from the sun, we have autumn and winter.

Challenge 6
(A) is loudest, as it is next to the source of the sound.

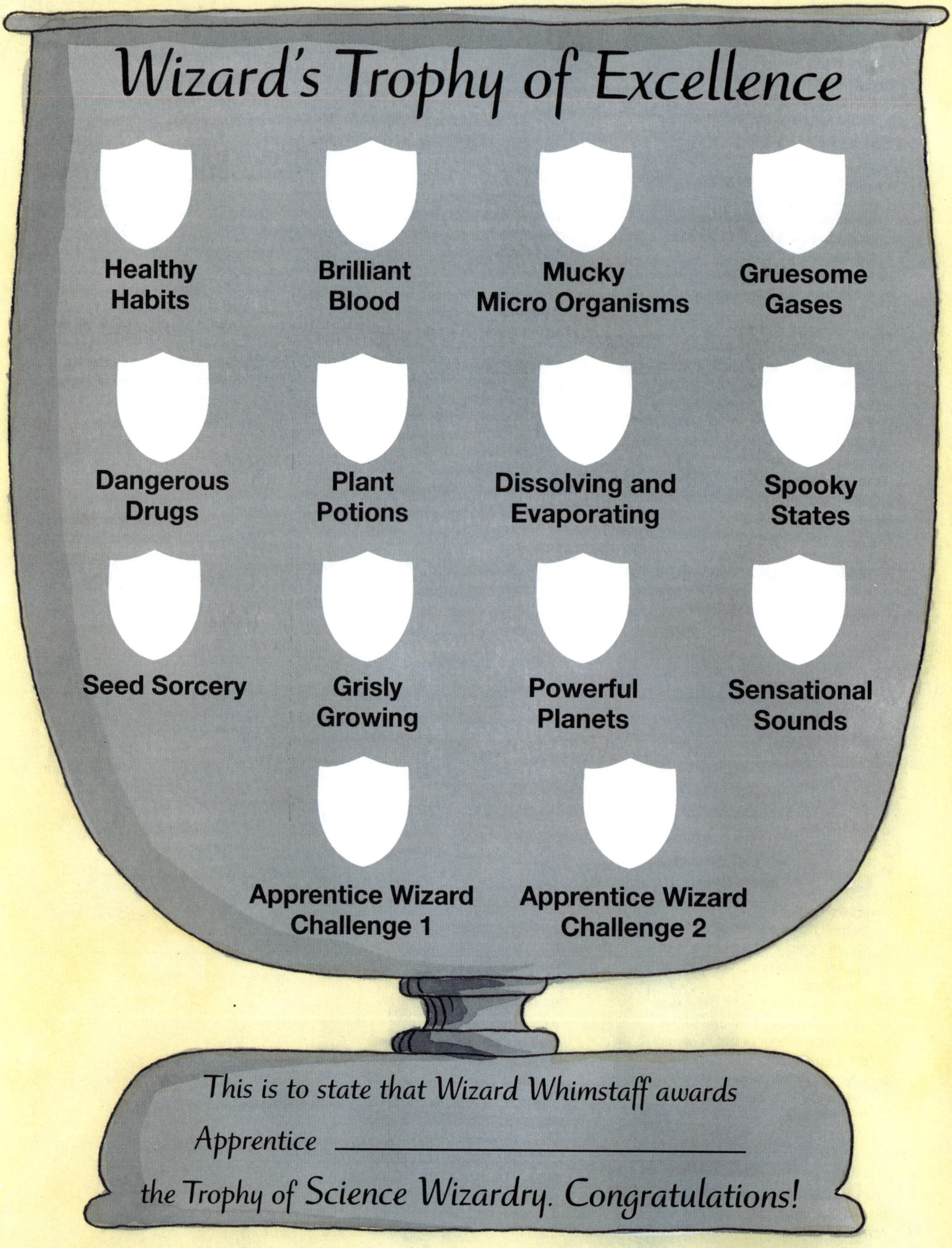

Wizard's Trophy of Excellence

Healthy Habits

Brilliant Blood

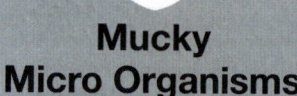
Mucky Micro Organisms

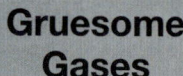
Gruesome Gases

Dangerous Drugs

Plant Potions

Dissolving and Evaporating

Spooky States

Seed Sorcery

Grisly Growing

Powerful Planets

Sensational Sounds

Apprentice Wizard Challenge 1

Apprentice Wizard Challenge 2

This is to state that Wizard Whimstaff awards Apprentice _____ the Trophy of Science Wizardry. Congratulations!

Published 2003

Letts Educational, The Chiswick Centre,
414 Chiswick High Road, London W4 5TF
Tel 020 8996 3333   Fax 020 8742 8390
Email mail@lettsed.co.uk
www.letts-education.com

Text, design and illustrations © Letts Educational Ltd 2003

Author: Lynn Huggins-Cooper
Book Concept and Development:
Helen Jacobs, Publishing Director; Sophie London, Project Editor
Design and Editorial: 2idesign ltd, Cambridge
Cover Design: Linda Males
Illustrations: Mike Phillips (Beehive Illustration)
Cover Illustration: Neil Chapman (Beehive Illustration)

Letts Educational Limited is a division of Granada Learning Limited. Part of Granada plc.

All rights reserved. No part of this publication may be reproduced, stored in a retrieval system, or transmitted, in any form or by any means, electronic, mechanical, photocopying, recording or otherwise, without the prior permission of Letts Educational.

British Library Cataloguing in Publication Data

A CIP record for this book is available from the British Library.

ISBN 1 84315 133 2

Printed in Italy

Colour reproduction by PDQ Repro Limited, Bungay, Suffolk.